I CAN'T WAIT TO CANCEL THIS

A Planner for People Who Don't Like People

BETH EVANS

MORROW
GIFT

this diary belongs to:

I CAN'T
WAIT TO
CANCEL THIS

important dates

_____

_____

_____

_____

notes

_____

_____

_____

_____

goals

_____

_____

_____

_____

JANUARY

a time to convince myself I will get it all done, but I will probably just ignore it

JANUARY

monday

tuesday

wednesday

thursday

friday

saturday | sunday

JANUARY

monday

tuesday

wednesday

thursday

friday

saturday | sunday

JANUARY

monday

tuesday

wednesday

thursday

friday

saturday | sunday

JANUARY

monday

tuesday

wednesday

thursday

friday

saturday | sunday

JANUARY

monday

tuesday

wednesday

thursday

friday

saturday | sunday

important dates

_____

_____

_____

_____

notes

_____

_____

_____

_____

goals

_____

_____

_____

_____

FEBRUARY

love
love
love
love

oh how
I love to hate it

FEBRUARY

monday

tuesday

wednesday

thursday

friday

saturday | sunday

FEBRUARY

monday

tuesday

wednesday

thursday

friday

saturday | sunday

FEBRUARY

monday

tuesday

wednesday

thursday

friday

saturday | sunday

FEBRUARY

monday

tuesday

wednesday

thursday

friday

saturday | sunday

FEBRUARY

monday

tuesday

wednesday

thursday

friday

saturday | sunday

important dates

_____

_____

_____

_____

notes

_____

_____

_____

_____

goals

_____

_____

_____

_____

MARCH
SADNESS BRACKET

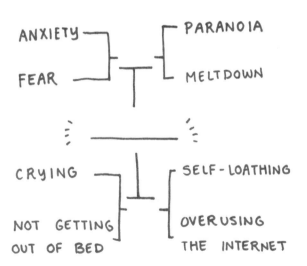

ANXIETY
FEAR

PARANOIA
MELTDOWN

CRYING
NOT GETTING OUT OF BED

SELF-LOATHING
OVERUSING THE INTERNET

MARCH

monday

tuesday

wednesday

thursday

friday

saturday | sunday

MARCH

monday

tuesday

wednesday

thursday

friday

saturday | sunday

MARCH

monday

tuesday

wednesday

thursday

friday

saturday | sunday

MARCH

monday

tuesday

wednesday

thursday

friday

saturday | sunday

MARCH

monday

tuesday

wednesday

hursday

friday

saturday | sunday

important dates

_____

_____

_____

_____

notes

_____

_____

_____

_____

goals

_____

_____

_____

_____

APRIL

where I
keep
hoping
it's spring

but
spring ends
up being
mostly rain

APRIL

monday

tuesday

wednesday

thursday

friday

saturday | sunday

APRIL

monday

tuesday

wednesday

thursday

friday

saturday | sunday

APRIL

monday

tuesday

wednesday

thursday

friday

saturday | sunday

APRIL

monday

tuesday

wednesday

thursday

friday

saturday | sunday

APRIL

monday

tuesday

wednesday

thursday

friday

saturday | sunday

important dates

_____

_____

_____

_____

notes

_____

_____

_____

_____

goals

_____

_____

_____

_____

MAY

a month where I remember everyone is moving on in life (except me)

MAY

monday

tuesday

wednesday

thursday

friday

saturday | sunday

MAY

monday

tuesday

wednesday

thursday

friday

saturday | sunday

MAY

monday

tuesday

wednesday

thursday

friday

saturday | sunday

MAY

monday

tuesday

wednesday

thursday

friday

saturday | sunday

MAY

monday

tuesday

wednesday

thursday

friday

saturday | sunday

important dates

_____

_____

_____

_____

notes

_____

_____

_____

_____

goals

_____

_____

_____

_____

JUNE

turns out
I can be
miserable
in nice weather too!

JUNE

monday

tuesday

wednesday

JUNE

monday

tuesday

wednesday

thursday

friday

saturday | sunday

JUNE

monday

tuesday

wednesday

thursday

friday

saturday | sunday

JUNE

monday

tuesday

wednesday

thursday

friday

saturday | sunday

JUNE

monday

tuesday

wednesday

thursday

friday

saturday | sunday

important dates

_____

_____

_____

_____

notes

_____

_____

_____

_____

goals

_____

_____

_____

_____

J U L Y

just gonna set aside
time for reading and
other personal - enrichment
projects and then just
end up scrolling on my
phone for hours

JULY

monday

tuesday

wednesday

thursday

friday

saturday | sunday

JULY

monday

tuesday

wednesday

thursday

friday

saturday | sunday

JULY

monday

tuesday

wednesday

thursday

friday

saturday | sunday

JULY

monday

tuesday

wednesday

thursday

friday

saturday | sunday

JULY

monday

tuesday

wednesday

thursday

friday

saturday | sunday

important dates

_____

_____

_____

_____

notes

_____

_____

_____

_____

goals

_____

_____

_____

_____

AUGUST

by now I have
melted into the
fabled Puddle of Sad

AUGUST

monday

tuesday

wednesday

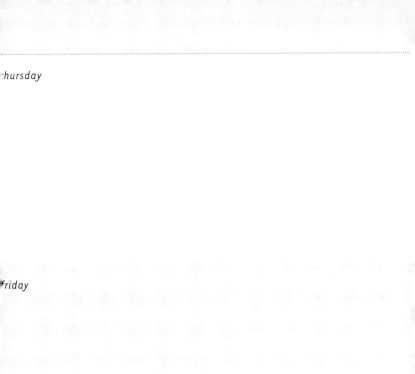

AUGUST

monday

tuesday

wednesday

thursday

friday

,

saturday | sunday

AUGUST

monday

tuesday

wednesday

thursday

friday

saturday | sunday

AUGUST

monday

tuesday

wednesday

hursday

riday

aturday / sunday

AUGUST

monday

tuesday

wednesday

thursday

friday

saturday | sunday

important dates

_____

_____

_____

_____

notes

_____

_____

_____

_____

goals

_____

_____

_____

_____

SEPTEMBER

FINALLY it's time to
trade in ill-fitting t-shirts

for
ill-fitting
sweatshirts

SEPTEMBER

monday

tuesday

wednesday

thursday

friday

saturday | sunday

SEPTEMBER

monday

tuesday

wednesday

thursday

friday

saturday | sunday

SEPTEMBER

monday

tuesday

wednesday

thursday

friday

saturday | sunday

SEPTEMBER

monday

tuesday

wednesday

thursday

friday

saturday | sunday

SEPTEMBER

monday

tuesday

wednesday

thursday

friday

saturday | sunday

important dates

_____

_____

_____

_____

notes

_____

_____

_____

_____

goals

_____

_____

_____

_____

OCTOBER

there's nothing scarier
than looking in the
mirror

and seeing
I have ZERO
self - esteem

OCTOBER

monday

tuesday

wednesday

thursday

friday

saturday | sunday

OCTOBER

monday

tuesday

wednesday

thursday

friday

saturday | sunday

OCTOBER

monday

tuesday

wednesday

thursday

friday

saturday | sunday

OCTOBER

monday

tuesday

wednesday

thursday

friday

saturday | sunday

OCTOBER

monday

tuesday

wednesday

thursday

friday

saturday | sunday

important dates

_____

_____

_____

_____

notes

_____

_____

_____

_____

goals

_____

_____

_____

_____

NOVEMBER

aka you
can't escape
the holidays

it's forced
interaction

AND

loneliness

wow

NOVEMBER

monday

tuesday

wednesday

thursday

friday

saturday | sunday

NOVEMBER

monday

tuesday

wednesday

thursday

friday

saturday | sunday

NOVEMBER

monday

tuesday

wednesday

thursday

friday

saturday | sunday

NOVEMBER

monday

tuesday

wednesday

thursday

friday

saturday | sunday

NOVEMBER

monday

tuesday

wednesday

thursday

friday

saturday | sunday

important dates

_____

_____

_____

_____

notes

_____

_____

_____

_____

goals

_____

_____

_____

_____

DECEMBER

please accept
these as a sign
I can occasionally
remember your
interests

DECEMBER

monday

tuesday

wednesday

thursday

friday

saturday | sunday

DECEMBER

monday

tuesday

wednesday

thursday

friday

saturday | sunday

DECEMBER

monday

tuesday

wednesday

thursday

friday

saturday | sunday

DECEMBER

monday

tuesday

wednesday

thursday

friday

saturday | sunday

DECEMBER

monday

tuesday

wednesday

thursday

friday

saturday | sunday

world time zones and international calling codes
(in case you need to discuss eurovision with your pals across the globe)

COUNTRY	INTERNATIONAL DIAL CODE	START GMT	END GMT	CAPITAL
Argentina	54	GMT-03:00		Buenos Aires
Australia	61	GMT+10:00	GMT+07:00	Sydney
Belgium	32	GMT+01:00		Brussels
Brazil	55	GMT-03:00	GMT-05:00	Brasilia
Bulgaria	359	GMT+02:00		Sofia
Canada	1	GMT-04:00	GMT-08:00	Ottawa
China	86	GMT+08:00		Beijing
Colombia	57	GMT-5:00		Bogota
Croatia	385	GMT+01:00		Zagreb
Czech Republic	420	GMT+01:00		Prague
Denmark	45	GMT+01:00		Copenhagen
Egypt	20	GMT+02:00		Cairo
Estonia	372	GMT+03:00		Tallinn
Finland	358	GMT+02:00		Helsinki
France	33	GMT+01:00		Paris
Germany	49	GMT+01:00		Berlin
Ghana	233	GMT		Accra
Gibraltar	350	GMT+01:00		Gibraltar
Greece	30	GMT+02:00		Athens
Hong Kong	852	GMT+08:00		Victoria City
Hungary	36	GMT+01:00		Budapest
Iceland	354	GMT		Reykjavík
India	91	GMT+05:30		New Delhi
Indonesia	62	GMT+7:00		Jakarta
Ireland	353	GMT		Dublin

Country	Code	GMT	GMT (alt)	City
Israel	972	GMT+02:00		Jerusalem
Italy	39	GMT+01:00		Rome
Japan	81	GMT+09:00		Tokyo
Kenya	254	GMT+03:00		Nairobi
Luxembourg	352	GMT+01:00		Luxembourg
Malaysia	60	GMT+08:00		Kuala Lumpur
Malta	356	GMT+01:00		Valletta
Mexico	52	GMT-06:00	GMT-08:00	Mexico City
Netherlands	31	GMT+01:00		Amsterdam
New Zealand	64	GMT+12:00		Wellington
Nigeria	234	GMT+01:00		Abuja
Poland	48	GMT+01:00		Warsaw
Portugal	351	GMT+01:00		Lisbon
Romania	40	GMT+02:00		Bucharest
Russia	7	GMT+03:00		Moscow
Saudi Arabia	966	GMT+03:00		Riyadh
Singapore	65	GMT+08:00		Singapore
South Africa	27	GMT+02:00		Pretoria
Spain	34	GMT+01:00		Madrid
Sri Lanka	94	GMT+05:30		Colombo
Sweden	46	GMT+01:00		Stockholm
Switzerland	41	GMT+01:00		Bern
Taiwan	886	GMT+08:00		Taipei
Thailand	66	GMT+07:00		Bangkok
Turkey	90	GMT+2:00		Ankara
United Kingdom	44	GMT		London
USA	1	GMT-05:00	GMT-11:00	Washington, DC
Zimbabwe	263	GMT+02:00		Harare

conversions tables/charts

(in case you feel like doing math or something)

DIMENSION	TO CONVERT	MULTIPLY BY	DIMENSION	TO CONVERT	MULTIPLY BY
LENGTH	inches (in) to millimeters (mm)	25	CAPACITY/ VOLUME	cu in to cu cm (cm^3)	16.387
	inches to centimeters (cm)	2.54		cu ft to cu meters (m^3)	0.0283
	feet (ft) to meters (m)	0.3048		cu yd to cu meters	0.7646
	yards (yd) to meters	0.9144		cu in to liters (l)	0.0164
	miles to kilometers (km)	1.6093		gallons to liters	4.5461
	millimeters to inches	0.0394		cu cm to cu in	0.061
	centimeters to inches	0.3937		cu meters to cu ft	35.3147
	meters to feet	3.2808		cu meters to cu yd	1.308
	meters to yards	1.0936		liters to cu in	61.0237
	kilometers to miles	0.6214		liters to gallons	0.22
AREA	sq in to sq cm (cm^2)	6.4516	WEIGHT/ MASS	grains to grams (g)	0.0648
	sq ft to sq meters (m^2)	0.0929		pounds (lb) to grams	453.5924
	sq yd to sq meters	0.8361		ounces (oz) to grams	28.3495
	sq miles to sq km (km^2)	2.59		pounds to kilograms (kg)	0.4536
	acres to hectares	0.4047		tons to kilograms	1016.0469
	sq cm to sq in	0.155		tons to tonnes (t)	1.016
	sq meters to sq ft	10.7639		grams to grains	15.4324
	sq meters to sq yd	1.196		grams to pounds	0.0022
	sq km to sq miles	0.3861		grams to ounces	0.3527
	hectares to acres	2.4711		kilograms to pounds	2.2046
				kilograms to tons	0.001
				tonnes to tons	0.9842

phonetic alphabet
(n case you need to talk in code)

A	Alpha	J	Juliet	S	Sierra		
B	Bravo	K	Kilo	T	Tango		
C	Charlie	L	Lima	U	Uniform		
D	Delta	M	Mike	V	Victor		
E	Echo	N	November	W	Whiskey		
F	Foxtrot	O	Oscar	X	X-Ray		
G	Golf	P	Papa	Y	Yankee		
H	Hotel	Q	Quebec	Z	Zulu		
I	India	R	Romeo				

wedding anniversary gifts
(in case you or someone you know got hitched at some point)

1st	paper	13th	pearl
2nd	cotton	14th	coral
3rd	leather	15th	crystal
4th	fruit/flowers/books	20th	china
5th	wood	25th	silver
6th	sugar/iron	30th	pearl
7th	wool/copper	35th	coral
8th	bronze	40th	ruby
9th	pottery	45th	sapphire
10th	tin	50th	gold
11th	china	55th	emerald
12th	silver	60th	diamond

roman numerals
(in case you go suddenly find yourself in the year 1100 BC)

1	I	13	XIII	70	LXX
2	II	14	XIV	80	LXXX
3	III	15	XV	90	XC
4	IV	16	XVI	100	C
5	V	17	XVII	200	CC
6	VI	18	XVIII	400	CD
7	VII	19	XIX	500	D
8	VIII	20	XX	600	DC
9	IX	30	XXX	700	DCC
10	X	40	XL	800	DCCC
11	XI	50	L	900	CM
12	XII	60	LX	1000	M

birthdays
(in case you want to celebrate your friends)

JANUARY	
FEBRUARY	
MARCH	
APRIL	
MAY	
JUNE	
JULY	
AUGUST	
SEPTEMBER	
OCTOBER	
NOVEMBER	
DECEMBER	

contacts
(in case you want to stay in touch)

Name
....

Address
....

Phone Number
....

Cell Phone
....

Email
....

Name
....

Address
....

Phone Number
....

Cell Phone
....

Email
....

Name
....

Address
....

Phone Number
....

Cell Phone
....

Email
....

Name

Address

Phone Number

Cell Phone

Email

Name

Address

Phone Number

Cell Phone

Email

Name

Address

Phone Number

Cell Phone

Email

contacts
(in case you want to stay in touch)

Name
....

Address
....

Phone Number
....

Cell Phone
....

Email
....

Name
....

Address
....

Phone Number
....

Cell Phone
....

Email
....

Name
....

Address
....

Phone Number
....

Cell Phone
....

Email
....

Name
....

Address
....

Phone Number
....

Cell Phone
....

Email
....

Name
....

Address
....

Phone Number
....

Cell Phone
....

Email
....

Name
....

Address
....

Phone Number
....

Cell Phone
....

Email
....

I CAN'T WAIT TO CANCEL THIS. Copyright © 2019 by Beth Evans. All rights reserved. Printed in China. No part of this book may be used or reproduced in any manner whatsoever without written permission except in the case of brief quotations embodied in critical articles and reviews. For information, address HarperCollins Publishers, 195 Broadway, New York, NY 10007.

HarperCollins books may be purchased for educational, business, or sales promotional use. For information, please email the Special Markets Department at SPsales@harpercollins.com.

FIRST EDITION

Designed by Bonni Leon-Berman

Library of Congress Cataloging-in-Publication Data has been applied for.

ISBN 978-0-06-279608-0

19 20 21 22 23   sc   10 9 8 7 6 5 4 3 2 1